No-Churn Ice Cream Cookbook

Quick and Easy Homemade No-Churn Ice Cream, Sundae Sauce, and Cone Recipes

Louise Davidson

All rights reserved © 2020 by Louise Davidson and The Cookbook Publisher. No part of this publication or the information in it may be quoted from or reproduced in any form by means such as printing, scanning, photocopying, or otherwise without prior written permission of the copyright holder.

This book is presented solely for motivational and informational purposes. The author and the publisher do not hold any responsibility for errors, omissions, or contrary interpretation of the subject matter herein.

The recipes provided in this book are for informational purposes only and are not intended to provide dietary advice. A medical practitioner should be consulted before making any changes in diet. Additionally, recipes' cooking times may require adjustment depending on age and quality of appliances. Readers are strongly urged to take all precautions to ensure ingredients are fully cooked to avoid the dangers of foodborne illnesses. The recipes and suggestions provided in this book are solely the opinions of the author. The author and publisher do not take any responsibility for any consequences that may result due to following the instructions provided in this book.

All the nutritional information contained in this book is provided for informational purposes only. This information is based on the specific brands, ingredients, and measurements used to make the recipe, and therefore the nutritional information is an estimate, and in no way is intended to be a guarantee of the actual nutritional value of the recipe made in the reader's home. The author and the publisher will not be responsible for any damages resulting in your reliance on the nutritional information. The best method to obtain an accurate count of the nutritional value in the recipe is to calculate the information with your specific brands, ingredients, and measurements.

ISBN: **9798694649872**

Printed in the United States

CONTENTS

INTRODUCTION	1
CLASSIC FLAVORS	3
FRUIT-BASED FLAVORS	31
NEW FLAVORS	67
COMBINATION FLAVORS	81
SUNDAE SAUCES	105
HOMEMADE CONES AND ICE CREAM	
SANDWICH COOKIES	111
RECIPE INDEX	119

INTRODUCTION

This ice cream cookbook is for all those ice cream lovers who really want to chill during the hot summer days or any time of the year! If you came this far to make ice cream all by yourself you are going to love this cookbook. Not because it's loaded with original flavors, but also you will find sundae sauces – and even recipes for homemade cones.

But the best part of the book is that it's for everybody – all the recipes are made without an ice cream machine, so whether you have one or not, you can enjoy the creamy delicious, and super tasty summer ice cream flavors that will chill you out. Also, the ingredients are all common and you probably have them in your kitchen right now!

The sundae sauces are delicious, and we recommend you to try them all. Choose from the very classic caramel sauce to chocolate, banana flavor, and also there is a healthier and fruitier version with strawberries.

All the ice cream recipes are inspired by favorite childhood flavors, many of which are also trendy nowadays, so you have a lot of options here. For example, if you crave a French toast for breakfast, I have a perfect French Toast Ice Cream recipe for all of you picky eaters out there. Also, there is a perfect Chai Tea inspired recipe, and I think you will all agree with me that we can't resist Pistachio Ice Cream.

Don't forget to make your own cones or sandwich cookies to enjoy the ice cream recipes as well!

All the ice cream recipes included in this cookbook will take between 10 to 16 minutes to prepare and have 6 ingredients or less. Talk about quick and easy! In a few steps, you will have delicious ice cream to share with your love ones... or keep for yourself!

The steps to make some no-churn ice cream include:
1. Gather your ingredients
2. Mix your ingredients
3. Pour in a freezer-safe container
4. Place in the freezer for 4 hours
5. Enjoy!

As far as equipment needed, only a freezer-safe container in Pyrex or stainless steel, an electric beater or whisk, and that's it!

Let's get started!

UK heavy cream is Double Cream
UK Cup is 250mL
14oz Sweetened Condensed milk is - 396.8 grams

CLASSIC FLAVORS

Vanilla Ice Cream

Vanilla is the World's favorite ice cream flavor!

*Serves 8 / Prep. time 10 minutes /
Freezing time 3 hours*

Ingredients
1 (14-ounce) can sweetened condensed milk
1 vanilla pod, scraped
1 teaspoon pure vanilla extract
2 cups heavy cream

Directions
1. In a large mixing bowl, combine the condensed milk, scraped vanilla from the pod, and vanilla extract.
2. In another bowl, whip the heavy cream until stiff peaks form.
3. Fold a scoop of the whipped cream into the condensed milk mixture, then transfer the sweetened condensed milk mixture into the remaining whipped cream and fold it in until it is creamy and delicious.
4. Spread the mixture in a Pyrex or stainless steel 8x8-inch pan.
5. Place the ice cream in the freezer for about 4 hours.

6. Remove the ice cream from the freezer and let it stand for 10 minutes.
7. Scoop out and serve.

Nutrition (per serving)
Calories 265, Fat 15.4 g, carbs 28 g, sugar 27.1 g
Protein 4.6 g, sodium 75 mg

Chocolate Ice Cream

If you are a chocolate lover, you are going to love this recipe!

Serves 12 I Prep. time 10 minutes I Freezing time 4 hours

Ingredients
¾ cup dark cocoa powder
1 (14-ounce) can sweetened condensed milk
1 teaspoon pure vanilla extract
2 cups heavy cream

Directions
1. In a large mixing bowl, combine the cocoa powder, condensed milk, and vanilla extract.
2. In another bowl, whip the heavy cream until stiff peaks form.
3. Fold a scoop of the whipped cream into the condensed milk mixture, then transfer the sweetened condensed milk mixture into the remaining whipped cream and fold it in until it is creamy and delicious.
4. Spread the mixture in a Pyrex or stainless steel 8x8-inch pan.
5. Place the ice cream in the freezer for about 4 hours.
6. Remove the ice cream from the freezer and let it stand for 10 minutes.

7. Scoop out and serve.

Nutrition (per serving)

Calories 278, Fat 18.2 g, carbs 27 g, sugar 24.2 g
Protein 4.8 g, sodium 120.1 mg

Strawberry Ice Cream

This next flavor the kids will love it the most. You can make it easy without any extra effort in the kitchen.

Serves 8 / Prep. time 10 minutes / Freezing time 3 hours

Ingredients
1 (14-ounce) can sweetened condensed milk
2 cups fresh or frozen strawberries, diced
1 teaspoon pure vanilla extract
2 cups heavy cream

Directions
1. In a large mixing bowl mix the condensed milk, diced strawberries, and vanilla extract.
2. In another bowl, whip the heavy cream until stiff peaks form.
3. Fold a scoop of the whipped cream into the condensed milk mixture, then transfer the sweetened condensed milk mixture into the remaining whipped cream and fold it in until it is creamy and delicious.
4. Spread the mixture in a Pyrex or stainless steel 8x8-inch pan.
5. Place the ice cream in the freezer for about 2 hours.

6. Take out the ice cream and fold in the diced strawberries. Return the pan to the freezer and freeze for 2 more hours.
7. Remove the ice cream from the freezer and let it stand for 10 minutes.
8. Scoop out and serve.

Nutrition (per serving)
Calories 277, Fat 15.4 g, carbs 31 g, sugar 29.3 g
Protein 4.5 g, sodium 74 mg

Butter Pecan Ice Cream

This classic flavor is super delicious! I am sure that a lot of you will agree that this delicious ice cream recipe is one of the best ice creams you have ever tried.

Serves 12 I Prep. time 15 minutes I Freezing time 4 hours

Ingredients
1 (14-ounce) can sweetened condensed milk
1 teaspoon vanilla extract
2 tablespoons melted butter
2 cups heavy cream
1 cup chopped pecans

Directions
1. In a large mixing bowl, combine the condensed milk, vanilla extract, and melted butter.
2. In another bowl, whip the chilled heavy cream until stiff peaks form.
3. Take one scoop of the whipped cream and fold it in the condensed milk mixture, then transfer the sweetened condensed milk mixture into the remaining whipped cream. Mix gently until it is creamy and delicious.
4. Pour the ice cream base into a Pyrex or stainless steel 8x8-inch pan, and place it in the freezer for about 2 hours.

5. Remove the pan from the freezer and fold in the chopped pecans, reserving some for the topping, if desired.
6. Return the ice cream to the freezer for about 2 more hours.
7. Remove the ice cream from the freezer and let it stand for 10 minutes.
8. Scoop out and serve.

Nutrition (per serving)
Calories 353, Fat 26.7 g, carbs 26 g, sugar 24.6 g
Protein 4.7 g, sodium 68.7 mg

Coffee Ice Cream

This is ice cream for coffee lovers! We don't recommend having it for breakfast, but it will get you on your feet!

Serves 12 / Prep. time 15 minutes / Freezing time 4 hours

Ingredients
1 cup brewed espresso
1 (14-ounce) can sweetened condensed milk
1 teaspoon pure vanilla extract
2 cups heavy cream
3 tablespoons chocolate sauce

Directions
1. In a large mixing bowl, combine the espresso with the sweetened condensed milk and vanilla extract.
2. In another bowl, whip the heavy cream until stiff peaks form.
3. Fold a scoop of the whipped cream into the condensed milk mixture, then transfer the sweetened condensed milk mixture into the remaining whipped cream and fold it in until it is creamy and delicious.
4. Spread the mixture in a Pyrex or stainless steel 8x8-inch pan.
5. Place the ice cream in the freezer for about 2 hours.

6. Swirl the chocolate sauce into the ice cream base and return it to the freezer for 2 more hours.
7. Remove the ice cream from the freezer and let it stand for 10 minutes.
8. Scoop out and serve.

Nutrition (per serving)
Calories 282, Fat 17.7 g, carbs 27.4 g, sugar 27g
Protein 3.8 g, sodium 62.3 mg

Coconut Ice Cream

This is a refreshing ice cream recipe that bursts with coconut flavor. All you have to do is to enjoy this natural flavor and share it with family and friends.

Serves 12 / Prep. time 15 minutes / Freezing time 4 hours

Ingredients
1 (14-ounce) can sweetened condensed milk
½ cup coconut flakes (plus more to garnish, optional) 50 grms
1 teaspoon pure vanilla extract
2 cups chilled heavy cream, chilled

Directions
1. In a large mixing bowl, combine the condensed milk with the coconut flakes and vanilla extract.
2. In another bowl, whip the heavy cream until stiff peaks form.
3. Fold a scoop of the whipped cream into the condensed milk mixture, then transfer the sweetened condensed milk mixture into the remaining whipped cream and fold it in until it is creamy and delicious.
4. Pour the mixture into a Pyrex or stainless steel 8x8-inch pan.

5. If you like, you can use an additional 2 or 3 tablespoons of toasted coconut to top the ice cream.
6. Place the ice cream base in the freezer for about 4 hours.
7. Remove the ice cream from the freezer and let it stand for 10 minutes.
8. Scoop out and serve.

Nutrition (per serving)

Calories 292, Fat 19.9 g, carbs 25 g, sugar 24.4 g Protein 4.0 g, sodium 56.2 mg

Chocolate Chip Ice Cream

A long-time favorite! If you cannot choose between vanilla and chocolate, this is the perfect flavor for you!

Serves 8 / Prep. time 10 minutes / Freezing time 3 hours

Ingredients
1 (14-ounce) can sweetened condensed milk
1 vanilla pod, scraped
1 teaspoon pure vanilla extract
2 cups heavy cream
¾ cup semi-sweet chocolate chips = 255 grams

Directions
1. In a large mixing bowl, combine the condensed milk, scraped vanilla from the pod, and vanilla extract.
2. In another bowl, whip the heavy cream until stiff peaks form.
3. Fold a scoop of the whipped cream into the condensed milk mixture, then transfer the sweetened condensed milk mixture into the remaining whipped cream and fold it in until it is creamy and delicious.
4. Pour the ice cream base into a Pyrex or stainless steel 8x8-inch pan, and place it in the freezer for about 2 hours.

5. Remove the pan from the freezer and fold in the chocolate chips.
6. Return the ice cream to the freezer for about 2 more hours.
7. Remove the ice cream from the freezer and let it stand for 10 minutes.
8. Scoop out and serve.

Nutrition (per serving)
Calories 265, Fat 15.4 g, carbs 27.8 g, sugar 27 g Protein 4.6 g, sodium 75 mg

Maple Walnut Ice Cream

Maple walnut is my mom's favorite flavors. It doesn't last long when she comes over!

Serves 12 I Prep. time 15 minutes I Cooking time 4-6 minutes I Freezing time 4 hours

Ingredients
2 cups walnuts, chopped
2 cups unsweetened evaporated milk
1 ½ cups maple syrup
2 cups heavy cream

Directions
1. Over medium-low heat, add the walnuts to a large non-stick pan. Stir-fry for about 4-6 minutes until golden and fragrant. Remove from heat and let cool.
2. In a large mixing bowl, combine the maple syrup and evaporated milk. Stir to combine.
3. In another bowl, whip the heavy cream until stiff peaks form.
4. Fold a scoop of the whipped cream into the maple mixture, then transfer them into the remaining whipped cream and fold it in until it is creamy. Taste and adjust sweetness with more maple syrup if needed.
5. Spread the mixture in a Pyrex or stainless steel 8x8-inch pan.

6. Place the ice cream in the freezer for about 2 hours.
7. Take out the ice cream and fold in the walnuts. Return the pan to the freezer and freeze for 2 more hours.
8. Remove the ice cream from the freezer and let it stand for 10 minutes.
9. Scoop out and serve.

Nutrition (per serving)
Calories 312, Fat 21.4 g, carbs 27.1 g, sugar 24 g
Protein 9.1 g, sodium 96 mg

Birthday Cake Ice Cream

Who doesn't love sprinkles in their ice cream? This birthday cake ice cream recipe will bring all the joy you need during the summer.

Serves 12 I Prep. time 15 minutes I Freezing time 4 hours

Ingredients
1 (14-ounce) can sweetened condensed milk
1 teaspoon vanilla extract
2 cups heavy cream
½ cup confetti sprinkles
¾ cup white sponge cake, crumbled

Directions
1. In a large mixing bowl, combine the sweetened condensed milk and vanilla extract.
2. In another bowl, whip the heavy cream until stiff peaks form.
3. Fold a scoop of the whipped cream into the condensed milk mixture, then transfer the sweetened condensed milk mixture into the remaining whipped cream and fold it in until it is creamy and delicious.
4. Spread the mixture in a Pyrex or stainless steel 8x8-inch pan.
5. Place the ice cream in the freezer for about 2 hours.

6. Take the ice cream out and fold the sprinkles and cake into the base. Return it to the freezer for another 2 hours.
7. Remove the ice cream from the freezer and let it stand for 10 minutes.
8. Scoop out and serve.

Nutrition (per serving)
Calories 329, Fat 19.1 g, carbs 36.2 g, sugar 30 g
Protein 4.6 g, sodium 79 mg

Peanut Butter Ice Cream

An American classic that will absolutely amaze your taste buds, Try it with strawberry sundae sauce for an amazing mix of flavors!

Serves 12 I
Prep. time 15 minutes plus cooling time I
Freezing time 4 hours

Ingredients
¾ cup smooth peanut butter
1 (14-ounce) can sweetened condensed milk
2 cups heavy cream, chilled
1 teaspoon pure vanilla extract

Directions
1. In a saucepan, melt the peanut butter. Remove it from the heat and let it cool slightly, and then stir in the sweetened condensed milk and vanilla extract. Let it cool completely.
2. In another bowl, whip the heavy cream until stiff peaks form.
3. Fold a scoop of the whipped cream into the condensed milk mixture, then transfer the sweetened condensed milk mixture into the remaining whipped cream and fold it in until it is creamy and delicious.
4. Pour the mixture into a Pyrex or stainless steel 8x8-inch pan.

5. If you like, you can use additional 2 or 3 teaspoons of peanut butter to make decorative swirls on the top.
6. Place the ice cream in the freezer for about 4 hours.
7. Remove the ice cream from the freezer and let it stand for 10 minutes.
8. Scoop out and serve.

Nutrition (per serving)
Calories 363, Fat 25.8 g, carbs 27 g, sugar 25.9 g Protein 7.8 g, sodium 129.2 mg

Neapolitan Ice Cream

If you are a huge fan of chocolate, vanilla, and strawberries and you can't decide what you want at the moment, then this Neapolitan Ice cream recipe is for you!

Serves 12 I Prep. time 15 minutes I Freezing time 4 hours

Ingredients
1 (14-ounce) can sweetened condensed milk
1 teaspoon vanilla extract
2 cups heavy cream
½ cup cocoa powder - 45grms
½ cup strawberry purée

Directions
1. In a large mixing bowl, combine the condensed milk and vanilla extract.
2. In another bowl, whip the heavy cream until stiff peaks form.
3. Take a scoop of the whipped cream and fold it in the condensed milk mixture, then transfer the sweetened condensed milk mixture into the remaining whipped cream. Mix gently.
4. Divide the mixture into three equal portions.
5. Into one of the portions, stir the cocoa powder. In another, stir in the strawberry

purée. Leave the third one with just the vanilla flavor.
6. Pour all three mixtures in a Pyrex or stainless steel 8x8-inch pan, keeping the three rows distinct as best you can.
7. Place the ice cream in the freezer for about 4 hours.
8. Remove the ice cream from the freezer and let it stand for 10 minutes.
9. Scoop out and serve.

Nutrition (per serving)
Calories 279, Fat 18 g, carbs 26.8 g, sugar 24.7 g
Protein 4.6 g, sodium 56 mg

Pistachio Ice Cream

This is one of the best ice cream recipes I have developed so far, and I am sure that you are going to love it. It has a soft and smooth ice cream base with a crunch that comes from the chopped pistachios. This is sure to be one of your favorites from the whole book.

Serves 12 / Prep. time 15 minutes / Freezing time 4 hours

Ingredients
¾ cup pistachio paste
1 (14-ounce) can sweetened condensed milk
1 teaspoon pure vanilla extract
2 cups heavy cream
½ cup roasted chopped pistachios

Directions
1. In a large mixing bowl, combine the pistachio paste, condensed milk, and vanilla extract.
2. In another bowl, whip the heavy cream until stiff peaks form.
3. Fold a scoop of the whipped cream into the condensed milk mixture, then transfer the sweetened condensed milk mixture into the remaining whipped cream and fold it in until it is creamy and delicious.

4. Spread the mixture in a Pyrex or stainless steel 8x8-inch pan.
5. Place the ice cream in the freezer for about 2 hours.
6. Take out the ice cream and fold in the pistachios. Return the pan to the freezer and freeze for 2 more hours.
7. Remove the ice cream from the freezer and let it stand for 10 minutes.
8. Scoop out and serve.

Nutrition (per serving)
Calories 291, Fat 19.2 g, carbs 26 g, sugar 22.3 g Protein 6.2 g, sodium 76.3 mg

Chocolate Chip Cookie Dough Ice Cream

If you love chocolate chip cookies – and who doesn't – you'll enjoy this delicious chocolate chip cookie dough ice cream recipe. You can make the dough ahead and keep it in the freezer if you like.

Serves 12 / Prep. time 15 minutes / Freezing time 4 hours

Ingredients
For the cookie dough
¼ cup butter, softened - 240g
3 tablespoons brown sugar
2 tablespoons granulated sugar
1 tablespoon whole milk
1 teaspoon vanilla extract
⅓ cup all-purpose flour - 42g
⅓ cup chocolate chips - 113g

For the ice cream base
1 (14-ounce) can sweetened condensed milk
1 teaspoon vanilla extract
2 cups heavy cream

Directions
1. Make the cookie dough. In a large mixing bowl, beat the butter with the brown sugar and granulated sugar.

2. Stir in the whole milk, vanilla extract, and flour.
3. Finally, fold in the chocolate chips. Cover, and refrigerate.
4. Make the ice cream base. In a large mixing bowl, combine the sweetened condensed milk and vanilla extract.
5. In another bowl, whip the heavy cream until stiff peaks form.
6. Take a scoop of the whipped cream and fold it in the condensed milk mixture, then transfer the sweetened condensed milk mixture into the remaining whipped cream. Mix gently.
7. Pour the base into a Pyrex or stainless steel 8x8-inch pan, and freeze for 2 hours.
8. Remove the cookie dough mixture from the fridge and crumble it up with a fork. (You can form it into tiny balls, if desired.)
9. Take out the ice cream base and fold in the cookie dough pieces.
10. Place the ice cream back in the freezer for about 2 more hours.
11. Remove the ice cream from the freezer and let it stand for 10 minutes.
12. Scoop, and serve!

Nutrition (per serving)
Calories 365, Fat 23.4 g, carbs 37 g, sugar 33.1 g
Protein 4.6 g, sodium 88.4 mg

Mint and Chocolate Chip Ice Cream

You already know this flavor and I am sure that you are going to love making it. It can be enjoyed by any age and I am sure that it will be your go-to frozen dessert during the hot weather.

Serves 12 / Prep. time 15 minutes / Freezing time 4 hours

Ingredients
1 (14-ounce) can sweetened condensed milk
1 teaspoon vanilla extract
1 teaspoon mint extract
½ teaspoon green food coloring
2 cups heavy cream
1 cup mini chocolate chips

Directions
1. In a large mixing bowl, combine the condensed milk, vanilla extract, mint extract, and food coloring.
2. In another bowl, whip the chilled heavy cream until stiff peaks form.
3. Take one scoop of the whipped cream and fold it in the condensed milk mixture, then transfer the sweetened condensed milk mixture into the remaining whipped cream. Mix gently until it is creamy and delicious.

4. Pour the ice cream base into a Pyrex or stainless steel 8x8-inch pan, and place it in the freezer for about 2 hours.
5. Remove the pan from the freezer and fold in the chocolate chips, reserving some for the topping, if desired.
6. Return the ice cream to the freezer for about 2 more hours.
7. Remove the ice cream from the freezer and let it stand for 10 minutes.
8. Scoop out and serve.

Nutrition (per serving)
Calories 361, Fat 23 g, carbs 36.2 g, sugar 34.9 g
Protein 3.8 g, sodium 55.1 mg

FRUIT-BASED FLAVORS

Blackberry Lime Ice Cream

It's unusual, but this combination pairs well, I am here to say! You all need to try this combo and believe me; you are going to love it.

Serves 12 I Prep. time 15 minutes I Freezing time 4 hours

Ingredients
Juice and zest of 1 lime
1 (14-ounce) can sweetened condensed milk
1 teaspoon pure vanilla extract
2 cups heavy cream
2 cups blackberries, cleaned and mashed
2 tablespoons honey

Directions
1. In a large mixing bowl, combine the lime juice and zest with the condensed milk and vanilla extract.
2. In another bowl, whip the heavy cream until stiff peaks form.
3. Fold a scoop of the whipped cream into the condensed milk mixture, then transfer the sweetened condensed milk mixture into the remaining whipped cream and fold it in until it is creamy and delicious.

4. Spread the mixture in a Pyrex or stainless steel 8x8-inch pan.
5. Place the ice cream in the freezer for about 2 hours.
6. Meanwhile, combine the blackberries with the honey.
7. Fold the blackberries into the ice cream base and return it to the freezer for 2 more hours.
8. Remove the ice cream from the freezer and let it stand for 10 minutes.
9. Scoop out and serve.

Nutrition (per serving)
Calories 355, Fat 18.3 g, carbs 46 g, sugar 34.2 g
Protein 4.9 g, sodium 55.4 mg

Raspberry and Chocolate Ice Cream

If you are a true chocolate lover, but you also like fruit, then you are going to love this raspberry and chocolate ice cream recipe. It's super easy to make and it can be done with cherries as well.

Serves 12 I Prep. time 15 minutes I Freezing time 4 hours

Ingredients
¾ cup dark cocoa powder
1 (14-ounce) can sweetened condensed milk
1 teaspoon pure vanilla extract
2 cups heavy cream
1 ½ cups fresh or frozen raspberries

Directions
1. In a large mixing bowl, combine the cocoa powder, condensed milk, and vanilla extract.
2. In another bowl, whip the heavy cream until stiff peaks form.
3. Fold a scoop of the whipped cream into the condensed milk mixture, then transfer the sweetened condensed milk mixture into the remaining whipped cream and fold it in until it is creamy and delicious.
4. Spread the mixture in a Pyrex or stainless steel 8x8-inch pan.

5. Place the ice cream in the freezer for about 2 hours.
6. Take out the ice cream and fold in the raspberries. Return the pan to the freezer and freeze for 2 more hours.
7. Remove the ice cream from the freezer and let it stand for 10 minutes.
8. Scoop out and serve.

Nutrition (per serving)
Calories 285, Fat 18 g, carbs 28.9 g, sugar 24.9 g
Protein 5.0 g, sodium 120.1 mg

Pear Ice Cream

Even though pear is a fall fruit, you can enjoy this flavor during the summer. Fast, fresh, and refreshing.

Serves 12 / Prep. time 15 minutes / Freezing time 4 hours

Ingredients
2 ripe pears, peeled and cored
1 (14-ounce) can sweetened condensed milk
1 teaspoon pure vanilla extract
2 cups heavy cream, chilled

Directions
1. In a high-speed blender or food processor, purée the pears until smooth.
2. In a large mixing bowl, mix the condensed milk with the pear purée and vanilla extract.
3. In another bowl, whip the chilled heavy cream until stiff peaks form.
4. Fold a scoop of the whipped cream into the condensed milk mixture, then transfer the sweetened condensed milk mixture into the remaining whipped cream and fold it in until it is creamy and delicious.
5. Spread the mixture in a Pyrex or stainless steel 8x8-inch pan.
6. Place the ice cream in the freezer for about 4 hours.

7. Remove the ice cream from the freezer and let it stand for 10 minutes.
8. Scoop out and serve.

Nutrition (per serving)
Calories 281, Fat 17.7 g, carbs 28 g, sugar 26.9 g
Protein 3.9 g, sodium 55.1 mg

Apple Caramel Ice Cream

Enjoy the natural fresh taste of the apples in this next recipe. You can substitute them with 1 cup of apple sauce, but if you have some fresh apples on your hands, they bring the best flavor to this recipe.

Serves 12 / Prep. time 15 minutes / Freezing time 4 hours

Ingredients
2 ripe apples, peeled and diced
1 (14 ounce) can sweetened condensed milk
1 teaspoon pure vanilla extract
2 cups heavy cream
½ cup caramel sauce, for topping

Directions
1. In a high-speed blender or food processor, purée the apples until smooth.
2. In a large mixing bowl, mix the condensed milk with the apple purée and vanilla extract.
3. In another bowl, whip the chilled heavy cream until stiff peaks form.
4. Fold a scoop of the whipped cream into the condensed milk mixture, then transfer the sweetened condensed milk mixture into the remaining whipped cream and fold it in until it is creamy and delicious.

5. Spread the mixture in a Pyrex or stainless steel 8x8-inch pan, and swirl the caramel sauce on the top.
6. Place the ice cream in the freezer for about 4 hours.
7. Remove the ice cream from the freezer and let it stand for 10 minutes.
8. Scoop out and serve.

Nutrition (per serving)
Calories 339, Fat 21.9 g, carbs 33 g, sugar 32.5 g Protein 4.0 g, sodium 56.7 mg

Honey Ice Cream

If you love the taste of honey, this yummy ice cream recipe is unique and refreshing on summer days with family and friends.

Serves 12 / Prep. time 10 minutes / Freezing time 4 hours

Ingredients
½ cup liquid honey, plus 2 tablespoons for topping
1 (14-ounce) can sweetened condensed milk
1 teaspoon pure vanilla extract
2 cups heavy cream, chilled

Directions
1. In a large mixing bowl, mix the ½ cup honey, condensed milk, and vanilla extract.
2. In another bowl, whip the heavy cream until stiff peaks form.
3. Fold a scoop of the whipped cream into the condensed milk mixture, then transfer the sweetened condensed milk mixture into the remaining whipped cream and fold it in until it is creamy and delicious.
4. Spread the mixture in a Pyrex or stainless steel 8x8-inch pan, and drizzle the 2 tablespoons of honey on top.
5. Place the ice cream in the freezer for about 4 hours.

6. Remove the ice cream from the freezer and let it stand for 10 minutes.
7. Scoop out and serve.

Nutrition (per serving)
Calories 311, Fat 17.7 g, carbs 36 g, sugar 35.8 g
Protein 3.9 g, sodium 55.7 mg

Chocolate Chips Ice Cream

This Stracciatella inspired Ice cream recipe, is not only easy to make but very enjoyable to eat and consume. Especially when it's consumed with family and friends.

Serves 4 / Prep. time 10 minutes / Freezing time 3 hours

Ingredients
1 cup chocolate chips
1 14 oz. can sweetened condensed milk
2 cups heavy cream
1 teaspoon pure vanilla extract

Directions
1. In a large mixing bowl mix the condensed milk with chocolate chips and vanilla extract.
2. In another bowl whip up the chilled heavy cream until stiff peaks.
3. Take a big scoop from the whipped cream and fold it in the condensed milk mixture.
4. Then, transfer the sweetened condensed milk mixture in the remaining whipped cream and fold in until creamy and delicious.
5. Pour the mixture in a Pyrex or stainless steel 9x13-inch pan.

6. If you like you can use an additional sprinkle of mini chocolate chips.
7. Place the ice cream base in the freezer for about 3 hours.
8. Remove the ice cream from the freezer and let it stand for 10 minutes.
9. Scoop out and serve.

Nutrition (per serving)
Calories 753, Fat 43 g, carbs 80.7 g, sugar 75.8 g
Protein 12.3 g, sodium 182 mg

Date Ice Cream

You are going to love this next date inspired recipe, that is sweetened by the natural sweet flavor of the dates. Easy to make, even easier to eat during the hot weather.

Serves 4 / Prep. time 10 minutes / Freezing time 3 hours

Ingredients
1 cup dates, finely chopped
1 14 oz. can sweetened condensed milk
2 cups heavy cream
1 teaspoon pure vanilla extract

Directions
1. In a large mixing bowl mix the condensed milk with chopped dates and vanilla extract.
2. In another bowl whip up the chilled heavy cream until stiff peaks.
3. Take a big scoop from the whipped cream and fold it in the condensed milk mixture.
4. Then, transfer the sweetened condensed milk mixture in the remaining whipped cream and fold in until creamy and delicious.
5. Pour the mixture in a Pyrex or stainless steel 9x13-inch pan.
6. If you like you can use an additional sprinkle of chopped dates.

7. Place the ice cream base in the freezer for about 3 hours.
8. Remove the ice cream from the freezer and let it stand for 10 minutes.
9. Scoop out and serve.

Nutrition (per serving)
Calories 654, fat 31g, carbs 89.2 g, sugar 82.4 g
Protein 10.2 g, sodium 150 mg

Almond Butter Ice Cream

Nutty in flavor, this next recipe, is not only more on the healthy side but very delicious. I am sure that you are going to enjoy it a lot.

Serves 4 / Prep. time 10 minutes / Freezing time 3 hours

Ingredients
¾ cup smooth almond butter
1 14 oz. can sweetened condensed milk
2 cups chilled heavy cream
1 teaspoon pure vanilla extract

Directions
1. In a large mixing bowl mix the condensed milk with melted almond butter and vanilla extract.
2. In another bowl whip up the chilled heavy cream until stiff peaks.
3. Take a big scoop from the whipped cream and fold it in the condensed milk mixture.
4. Then, transfer the sweetened condensed milk mixture in the remaining whipped cream and fold in until creamy and delicious.
5. Pour the mixture in a Pyrex or stainless steel 9x13-inch pan.

6. If you like you can use additional 2-3 teaspoons of almond butter and make swirls.
7. Place the ice cream base in the freezer for about 3 hours.
8. Remove the ice cream from the freezer and let it stand for 10 minutes.
9. Scoop out and serve.

Nutrition (per serving)
Calories 814, Fat 56 g, carbs 64.8 g, sugar 57.2 g Protein 18.1 g, sodium 149 mg

Cherry Ice Cream

This flavor is super refreshing and very simple to make. This one is without egg in the ice cream base, so you are going to love the simplicity of the way of preparing this ice cream recipe.

Serves 4 I Prep. time 10 minutes I Freezing time 3 hours

Ingredients
1 ½ cup frozen cherries, pitted
1 14 oz. can sweetened condensed milk
2 cups heavy cream
1 teaspoon pure vanilla extract

Directions
1. In a large mixing bowl mix the condensed milk, cherries, and vanilla extract.
2. In another bowl whip up the chilled heavy cream until stiff peaks.
3. Take a big scoop from the whipped cream and fold it in the condensed milk mixture.
4. Then, transfer the sweetened condensed milk mixture in the remaining whipped cream and fold in until creamy and delicious.
5. Pour the mixture in a Pyrex or stainless steel 9x13-inch pan.

6. If you like, at this point you can add cherries here and there in the ice cream base mixture.
7. Place the ice cream base in the freezer for about 3 hours.
8. Remove the ice cream from the freezer and let it stand for 10 minutes.
9. Scoop out and serve.

Nutrition (per serving)
Calories 555, Fat 31.1 g, carbs 62.2g, sugar 59.4 g
Protein 9.6 g, sodium 149 mg

Plum Chip Ice Cream

Make this delicious dessert when plums are in season and just bursting with rich, ripe flavor.

Serves 12 / Prep. time 15 minutes / Freezing time 4 hours

Ingredients
4 ripe plums, peeled and diced
1 (14-ounce) can sweetened condensed milk
1 teaspoon pure vanilla extract
2 cups heavy cream, chilled
1 cup mini chocolate chips

Directions
1. In a high-speed blender or food processor, purée the plums until smooth.
2. In a large mixing bowl, combine the condensed milk with plum purée and vanilla extract.
3. In another bowl, whip the heavy cream until stiff peaks form.
4. Fold one scoop of the whipped cream into the condensed milk mixture, and then transfer the sweetened condensed milk mixture into the remaining whipped cream and fold in until creamy and smooth.
5. Spread the mixture in a Pyrex or stainless steel 8x8-inch pan and freeze for 2 hours. Gently stir in the mini chocolate chips.

6. Freeze for 2 more hours.
7. Remove the ice cream from the freezer and let it stand for 10 minutes.
8. Scoop out and serve.

Nutrition (per serving)
Calories 372, Fat 23.1 g, carbs 38.7 g sugar 37.1 g
Protein 4.0 g, sodium 55.1 mg

Dried Fig Ice Cream

Are you craving dried figs? You can enjoy them in a completely new way – ice cream.

Serves 12 I Prep. time 24-26 minutes I Freezing time 4 hours

Ingredients
1 cup dried figs
¼ cup warm milk
1 (14-ounce) can sweetened condensed milk
1 teaspoon pure vanilla extract
2 cups heavy cream
½ cup finely chopped dried figs

Directions
1. Soak the figs in the warm milk for 15 minutes, and then purée until smooth.
2. In a large mixing bowl, combine the condensed milk with fig purée and vanilla extract.
3. In another bowl, whip the heavy cream until stiff peaks form.
4. Fold a scoop of the whipped cream into the condensed milk mixture, then transfer the sweetened condensed milk mixture into the remaining whipped cream and fold it in until it is creamy and delicious.
5. Spread the mixture in a Pyrex or stainless steel 8x8-inch pan.

6. Place the ice cream in the freezer for about 2 hours.
7. Fold in the remaining dried figs, and return to the freezer for 2 more hours.
8. Remove the ice cream from the freezer and let it stand for 10 minutes.
9. Scoop out and serve.

Nutrition (per serving)
Calories 332, Fat 18 g, carbs 40.3 g, sugar 36.4 g
Protein 4.8 g, sodium 59.8 mg

Banana Bread Ice Cream

If you like banana bread, then you are going to love this fruity flavor with a crunch of walnuts. Yummy, easy to make, and super refreshing during the summer.

Serves 12 / Prep. time 15 minutes / Freezing time 4 hours

Ingredients
2 bananas, mashed with a fork
½ teaspoon cinnamon
1 (14-ounce) can sweetened condensed milk
1 teaspoon pure vanilla extract
2 cups heavy cream
¼ cup chopped walnuts

Directions
1. In a large mixing bowl, combine the bananas, cinnamon, sweetened condensed milk, and vanilla extract.
2. In another bowl, whip the heavy cream until stiff peaks form.
3. Fold a scoop of the whipped cream into the condensed milk mixture, then transfer the sweetened condensed milk mixture into the remaining whipped cream and fold it in until it is creamy and delicious.
4. Spread the mixture in a Pyrex or stainless steel 8x8-inch pan.

5. Place the ice cream in the freezer for about 2 hours.
6. Take the ice cream out and fold the walnuts into the base. Return it to the freezer for another 2 hours.
7. Remove the ice cream from the freezer and let it stand for 10 minutes.
8. Scoop out and serve.

Nutrition (per serving)
Calories 302, Fat 19.4 g, carbs 29 g, sugar 26.7 g Protein 4.4 g, sodium 55.4 mg

Cherry Ice Cream

Summer is all about unforgettable flavors, and when I say unforgettable, I mean vanilla and cherries – a flavor match made in heaven.

Serves 12 / Prep. time 20 minutes / Freezing time 4 hours

Ingredients
1 (14-ounce) can sweetened condensed milk
2 teaspoons pure vanilla extract
2 cups heavy cream
2 cups cherries, pitted and chopped

Directions
1. In a large mixing bowl, combine the condensed milk with the vanilla extract.
2. In another bowl, whip the heavy cream until stiff peaks form.
3. Fold a scoop of the whipped cream into the condensed milk mixture, then transfer the sweetened condensed milk mixture into the remaining whipped cream and fold it in until it is creamy and delicious.
4. Spread the mixture in a Pyrex or stainless steel 8x8-inch pan.
5. Place the ice cream in the freezer for about 2 hours.
6. Fold in the chopped cherries, and return to the freezer for 2 more hours.

7. Remove the ice cream from the freezer and let it stand for 10 minutes.
8. Scoop out and serve.

Nutrition (per serving)
Calories 280, Fat 17.7 g, carbs 27 g, sugar 26.7 g
Protein 4.0 g, sodium 55.1 mg

Blueberry Lemon Ice Cream

This ice cream recipe is bursting with flavor and the colors are so pretty. You can make it with orange zest as well and it will work perfectly.

Serves 12 / Prep. time 15 minutes / Freezing time 4 hours

Ingredients
2 teaspoons lemon zest
1 (14-ounce) can sweetened condensed milk
1 teaspoon pure vanilla extract
2 cups heavy cream
1 cup fresh blueberries

Directions
1. In a large mixing bowl, combine the lemon zest, sweetened condensed milk, and vanilla extract.
2. In another bowl, whip the heavy cream until stiff peaks form.
3. Fold a scoop of the whipped cream into the condensed milk mixture, then transfer the sweetened condensed milk mixture into the remaining whipped cream and fold it in until it is creamy and delicious.
4. Spread the mixture in a Pyrex or stainless steel 8x8-inch pan.
5. Place the ice cream in the freezer for about 2 hours.

6. Take the ice cream out and fold the blueberries into the base. Return it to the freezer for another 2 hours.
7. Remove the ice cream from the freezer and let it stand for 10 minutes.
8. Scoop out and serve.

Nutrition (per serving)
Calories 275, Fat 17.7 g, carbs 25.9 g, sugar 25 g
Protein 3.9 g, sodium 55.8 mg

Creamy Orange Ice Cream

This next flavor is the one the kids will love the most. You can make it easily without any extra effort in the kitchen.

Serves 12 / Prep. time 15 minutes / Freezing time 4 hours

Ingredients
1 (14-ounce) can sweetened condensed milk
1 teaspoon vanilla extract
1 ½ teaspoons orange extract
½ teaspoon orange food coloring, if desired
2 cups heavy cream

Directions
1. In a large mixing bowl, combine the condensed milk, vanilla extract, orange extract, and food coloring, if using.
2. In another bowl, whip the chilled heavy cream until stiff peaks form.
3. Take one scoop of the whipped cream and fold it in the condensed milk mixture, then transfer the sweetened condensed milk mixture into the remaining whipped cream. Mix gently until it is creamy and delicious.
4. Pour the ice cream base into a Pyrex or stainless steel 8x8-inch pan, and place it in the freezer for about 4 hours.

5. Remove the ice cream from the freezer and let it stand for 10 minutes.
6. Scoop out and serve.

Nutrition (per serving)
Calories 268, Fat 17.7 g, carbs 24 g, sugar 24.2 g
Protein 3.8 g, sodium 55.1 mg

Strawberry and Graham Cracker Ice Cream

Crunchy, fruity, and rich ice cream recipe you are going to love! Make it this summer and enjoy with your family members and friends at the pool party, garden chats or just sitting in front of the TV.

Serves 12 I Prep. time 15 minutes I Freezing time 4 hours

Ingredients
1 (14-ounce) can sweetened condensed milk
1 teaspoon pure vanilla extract
2 cups heavy cream
2 cups chopped strawberries
3 ounces crushed graham crackers

Directions
1. In a large mixing bowl, combine the sweetened condensed milk and vanilla extract.
2. In another bowl, whip the heavy cream until stiff peaks form.
3. Fold a scoop of the whipped cream into the condensed milk mixture, then transfer the sweetened condensed milk mixture into the remaining whipped cream and fold it in until it is creamy and delicious.
4. Spread the mixture in a Pyrex or stainless steel 8x8-inch pan.

5. Place the ice cream in the freezer for about 2 hours.
6. Fold the chopped strawberries and graham cracker crumbs into the ice cream base and return it to the freezer for 2 more hours.
7. Remove the ice cream from the freezer and let it stand for 10 minutes.
8. Scoop out and serve.

Nutrition (per serving)
Calories 305, Fat 18.5 g, carbs 31 g, sugar 27.2 g Protein 4.5 g, sodium 89.1 mg

Lemon and Poppy Seed Ice Cream

You might have tried this combination in loaf or muffins, and it's just as good in ice cream!

*Serves 12 / Prep. time 15 minutes /
Freezing time 4 hours*

Ingredients
Zest of 2 lemons
Juice of 1 lemon
2 tablespoons poppy seeds
1 (14-ounce) can sweetened condensed milk
1 teaspoon pure vanilla extract
2 cups heavy cream

Directions
1. In a large mixing bowl, combine the lemon zest, lemon juice, poppy seeds, sweetened condensed milk, and vanilla extract.
2. In another bowl, whip the heavy cream until stiff peaks form.
3. Fold a scoop of the whipped cream into the condensed milk mixture, then transfer the sweetened condensed milk mixture into the remaining whipped cream and fold it in until it is creamy and delicious.
4. Spread the mixture in a Pyrex or stainless steel 8x8-inch pan.
5. Place the ice cream in the freezer for about 4 hours.

6. Remove the ice cream from the freezer and let it stand for 10 minutes.
7. Scoop out and serve.

Nutrition (per serving)
Calories 277, Fat 18.3 g, carbs 24.8 g, sugar 24 g Protein 9.9 g, sodium 55.5 mg

Papaya Tropics Ice Cream

Tropical, refreshing, and super easy to make, this Caribbean-inspired ice cream will make you crave more!

Serves 12 / Prep. time 15 minutes / Freezing time 4 hours

Ingredients
1 ripe papaya, peeled, seeded, and diced
1 (14-ounce) can sweetened condensed milk
½ teaspoon coconut extract
2 cups heavy cream
1 cup crushed pineapple, drained
¼ cup maraschino cherries, diced

Directions
1. In a high-speed blender or food processor, purée the papaya until smooth.
2. In a large mixing bowl, combine the condensed milk with papaya purée and coconut extract.
3. In another bowl, whip the heavy cream until stiff peaks form.
4. Fold one scoop of the whipped cream into the condensed milk mixture, and then transfer the sweetened condensed milk mixture into the remaining whipped cream and fold in until creamy and smooth.

5. Spread the mixture in a Pyrex or stainless steel 8x8-inch pan and freeze for 2 hours. Gently stir in the crushed pineapple and scatter the cherries on top.
6. Freeze for 2 more hours.
7. Remove the ice cream from the freezer and let it stand for 10 minutes.
8. Scoop out and serve.

Nutrition (per serving)
Calories 298, Fat 17.7 g, carbs 32 g, sugar 31.0 g
Protein 4.2 g, sodium 56.2 mg

NEW FLAVORS

Cereal Ice Cream

If you ever crave ice cream for breakfast, you will love this totally customizable ice cream recipe. It's super fresh, it's easy to make and it's full of flavor.

*Serves 12 / Prep. time 15 minutes /
Freezing time 4 hours*

Ingredients
1 (14-ounce) can sweetened condensed milk
1 teaspoon pure vanilla extract
2 cups heavy cream
¾ cup cereal of your choice (we used Grape Nuts)

Directions
1. In a large mixing bowl, combine the sweetened condensed milk and vanilla extract.
2. In another bowl, whip the heavy cream until stiff peaks form.
3. Fold a scoop of the whipped cream into the condensed milk mixture, then transfer the sweetened condensed milk mixture into the remaining whipped cream and fold it in until it is creamy and delicious.
4. Spread the mixture in a Pyrex or stainless steel 8x8-inch pan.

5. Place the ice cream in the freezer for about 2 hours.
6. Take the ice cream out, and fold the cereal into the base. Return it to the freezer for another 2 hours.
7. Remove the ice cream from the freezer and let it stand for 10 minutes.
8. Scoop out and serve.

Nutrition (per serving)
Calories 320, Fat 17.9 g, carbs 35 g, sugar 25.5 g
Protein 5.8 g, sodium 127.6 mg

Pecans and Molasses Ice Cream

This sounds unusual, but the flavors match up perfectly. The flavor from the molasses is balanced perfectly by the lovely crunch from the pecans.

Serves 12 / Prep. time 15 minutes / Freezing time 4 hours

Ingredients
½ cup molasses
1 (14-ounce) can sweetened condensed milk
1 teaspoon pure vanilla extract
2 cups heavy cream
¾ cup roasted pecans

Directions
1. In a large mixing bowl, combine the molasses with the condensed milk and vanilla extract.
2. In another bowl, whip the heavy cream until stiff peaks form.
3. Fold a scoop of the whipped cream into the condensed milk mixture, then transfer the sweetened condensed milk mixture into the remaining whipped cream and fold it in until it is creamy and delicious.
4. Spread the mixture in a Pyrex or stainless steel 8x8-inch pan.

5. Place the ice cream in the freezer for about 2 hours.
6. Fold the pecans into the ice cream base and return it to the freezer for 2 more hours.
7. Remove the ice cream from the freezer and let it stand for 10 minutes.
8. Scoop out and serve.

Nutrition (per serving)
Calories 342, Fat 21.3 g, carbs 35 g, sugar 34.6 g
Protein 4.3 g, sodium 60.2 mg

Marshmallow Ice Cream

You are going to love this next flavor. It's sweet and colorful.

Serves 12 / Prep. time 15 minutes / Freezing time 4 hours

Ingredients
½ cup marshmallow fluff
1 (14-ounce) can sweetened condensed milk
1 teaspoon pure vanilla extract
2 cups heavy cream
½ cup colored mini marshmallows, snipped in half

Directions
1. In a large mixing bowl, combine the marshmallow fluff, sweetened condensed milk, and vanilla extract.
2. In another bowl, whip the heavy cream until stiff peaks form.
3. Fold a scoop of the whipped cream into the condensed milk mixture, then transfer the sweetened condensed milk mixture into the remaining whipped cream and fold it in until it is creamy and delicious.
4. Spread the mixture in a Pyrex or stainless steel 8x8-inch pan.
5. Place the ice cream in the freezer for about 2 hours.

6. Take the ice cream out and fold the mini marshmallows into the base. Return it to the freezer for another 2 hours.
7. Remove the ice cream from the freezer and let it stand for 10 minutes.
8. Scoop out and serve.

Nutrition (per serving)
Calories 287, 17.7 g, carbs 28.9 g, sugar 27.2 g
Protein 3.9 g, sodium 58.1 mg

Greek Yoghurt and Maple Syrup Ice Cream

This sweet and creamy ice cream is rich and delicious. If you love maple, give it a try.

Serves 12 I Prep. time 15 minutes I Freezing time 4 hours

Ingredients
½ cup Greek yogurt
½ cup maple syrup
1 (14-ounce) can sweetened condensed milk
1 teaspoon pure vanilla extract
2 cups heavy cream

Directions
1. In a large mixing bowl, combine the Greek yogurt, maple syrup, sweetened condensed milk, and vanilla extract.
2. In another bowl, whip the heavy cream until stiff peaks form.
3. Fold a scoop of the whipped cream into the condensed milk mixture, then transfer the sweetened condensed milk mixture into the remaining whipped cream and fold it in until it is creamy and delicious.
4. Spread the mixture in a Pyrex or stainless steel 8x8-inch pan.
5. Place the ice cream in the freezer for about 4 hours.

6. Remove the ice cream from the freezer and let it stand for 10 minutes.
7. Scoop out and serve.

Nutrition (per serving)
Calories 311, Fat 18 g, carbs 33.6 g, sugar 32.8 g
Protein 4.2 g, sodium 62.5 mg

Chai Ice Cream

This yummy tea-inspired ice cream recipe will actually give you chills with its rich and sophisticated flavor.

Serves 12 I Prep. time 10 minutes I Freezing time 4 hours

Ingredients
½ cup strong chai tea
1 (14-ounce) can sweetened condensed milk
1 teaspoon pure vanilla extract
2 cups heavy cream

Directions
1. In a large mixing bowl, mix the tea, condensed milk, and vanilla extract.
2. In another bowl, whip the heavy cream until stiff peaks form.
3. Fold a scoop of the whipped cream into the condensed milk mixture, then transfer the sweetened condensed milk mixture into the remaining whipped cream and fold it in until it is creamy and delicious.
4. Spread the mixture in a Pyrex or stainless steel 8x8-inch pan.
5. Place the ice cream in the freezer for about 4 hours.
6. Remove the ice cream from the freezer and let it stand for 10 minutes.

7. Scoop out and serve.

Nutrition (per serving)
Calories 268, Fat 17.7 g, carbs 24 g, sugar 24.2 g
Protein 3.8 g, sodium 55.1 mg

PB and J Ice Cream

Love peanut butter and jam? Then this is one of the ice cream recipes you are going to love the most. One taste of the cool, creamy favorite will take you right back to your childhood.

Serves 12 / Prep. time 15 minutes / Freezing time 4 hours

Ingredients
¾ cup creamy peanut butter
1 (14-ounce) can sweetened condensed milk
1 teaspoon pure vanilla extract
2 cups heavy cream
½ cup strawberry or raspberry jam

Directions
1. In a large mixing bowl, combine the peanut butter, sweetened condensed milk, and vanilla extract.
2. In another bowl, whip the heavy cream until stiff peaks form.
3. Fold a scoop of the whipped cream into the condensed milk mixture, then transfer the sweetened condensed milk mixture into the remaining whipped cream and fold it in until it is creamy and delicious.
4. Spread the mixture in a Pyrex or stainless steel 8x8-inch pan.

5. Place the ice cream in the freezer for about 2 hours.
6. Take the ice cream out and swirl the strawberry jam into the base. Return it to the freezer for another 2 hours.
7. Remove the ice cream from the freezer and let it stand for 10 minutes.
8. Scoop out and serve.

Nutrition (per serving)
Calories 396, Fat 26 g, carbs 36.8 g, sugar 33.7 g Protein 7.3 g, sodium 125.1 mg

Cinnamon French Toast Ice Cream

Cinnamon French toast Is one of the best breakfasts you can have, but wait a minute. What about hot summer days? Oh, yes – you can enjoy that flavor in a frozen dessert like this no-churn ice cream!

Serves 12 I Prep. time 15 minutes I Freezing time 4 hours

Ingredients
2 teaspoons cinnamon
1 (14-ounce) can sweetened condensed milk
1 teaspoon pure vanilla extract
2 cups heavy cream
1 slice French toast, diced into small cubes

Directions
1. In a large mixing bowl, combine the cinnamon, sweetened condensed milk, and vanilla extract.
2. In another bowl, whip the heavy cream until stiff peaks form.
3. Fold a scoop of the whipped cream into the condensed milk mixture, then transfer the sweetened condensed milk mixture into the remaining whipped cream and fold it in until it is creamy and delicious.
4. Spread the mixture in a Pyrex or stainless steel 8x8-inch pan.

5. Place the ice cream in the freezer for about 2 hours.
6. Take the ice cream out and fold the French toast into the base. Return it to the freezer for another 2 hours.
7. Remove the ice cream from the freezer and let it stand for 10 minutes.
8. Scoop out and serve.

Nutrition (per serving)
Calories 281, Fat 18.3 g, carbs 25.8 g, sugar 24 g
Protein 4.2 g, sodium 81.2 mg

COMBINATION FLAVORS

Chocolate and Hazelnut Ice Cream

You are going to be asked over and over again for this recipe! It's so rich and satisfying.

Serves 12 / Prep. time 15 minutes / Freezing time 4 hours

Ingredients
½ cup cocoa powder
¼ cup chocolate hazelnut spread
1 (14-ounce) can sweetened condensed milk
1 teaspoon pure vanilla extract
2 cups heavy cream
½ cup roasted chopped hazelnuts

Directions
1. In a large mixing bowl, combine the cocoa powder, hazelnut spread, condensed milk, and vanilla extract.
2. In another bowl, whip the heavy cream until stiff peaks form.
3. Fold a scoop of the whipped cream into the condensed milk mixture, then transfer the sweetened condensed milk mixture into the remaining whipped cream and fold it in until it is creamy and delicious.
4. Spread the mixture in a Pyrex or stainless steel 8x8-inch pan.

5. Place the ice cream in the freezer for about 2 hours.
6. Take out the ice cream and fold in the hazelnuts. Return the pan to the freezer and freeze for 2 more hours.
7. Remove the ice cream from the freezer and let it stand for 10 minutes.
8. Scoop out and serve.

Nutrition (per serving)
Calories 375, Fat 24.8 g, carbs 35.3 g, sugar 31 g
Protein 6.5 g, sodium 125.1 mg

Almond Butter Ice Cream

This decadent flavor is really good if you want to enjoy your ice cream in a very elegant way! We recommend you read your favorite magazine or watch your favorite series while you have a bowl of this yummy ice cream.

Serves 12 I Prep. time 15 minutes I Freezing time 4 hours

Ingredients
¾ cup almond butter
1 (14-ounce) can sweetened condensed milk
1 teaspoon pure vanilla extract
2 cups heavy cream
½ cup chopped roasted almonds

Directions
1. In a large mixing bowl, combine the almond butter, condensed milk, and vanilla extract.
2. In another bowl, whip the heavy cream until stiff peaks form.
3. Fold a scoop of the whipped cream into the condensed milk mixture, then transfer the sweetened condensed milk mixture into the remaining whipped cream and fold it in until it is creamy and delicious.
4. Spread the mixture in a Pyrex or stainless steel 8x8-inch pan.

5. Place the ice cream in the freezer for about 2 hours.
6. Take out the ice cream and fold in the almonds. Return the pan to the freezer and freeze for 2 more hours.
7. Remove the ice cream from the freezer and let it stand for 10 minutes.
8. Scoop out and serve.

Nutrition (per serving)
Calories 387, Fat 28.5 g, carbs 28.4 g, sugar 25 g
Protein 7.1 g, sodium 56.9 mg

Peanut Butter and Chocolate Chip Ice Cream

Enjoy this American classic flavor in a delicious new way! Prepare it like ice cream and have fun eating it with your family and friends.

Serves 12 / Prep. time 15 minutes / Freezing time 4 hours

Ingredients
¾ cup smooth peanut butter
1 (14-ounce) can sweetened condensed milk
1 teaspoon pure vanilla extract
2 cups heavy cream
1 cup chocolate chips

Directions
1. In a large mixing bowl, combine the peanut butter, condensed milk, and vanilla extract.
2. In another bowl, whip the heavy cream until stiff peaks form.
3. Fold a scoop of the whipped cream into the condensed milk mixture, then transfer the sweetened condensed milk mixture into the remaining whipped cream and fold it in until it is creamy and delicious.
4. Spread the mixture in a Pyrex or stainless steel 8x8-inch pan.
5. Place the ice cream in the freezer for about 2 hours.

6. Take out the ice cream and fold in the chocolate chips. Return the pan to the freezer and freeze for 2 more hours.
7. Remove the ice cream from the freezer and let it stand for 10 minutes.
8. Scoop out and serve.

Nutrition (per serving)
Calories 456, Fat 31.8 g, carbs 39 g, sugar 36.6 g
Protein 9.2 g, sodium 142.5 mg

Peanut Butter and Banana Ice Cream

Banana and peanut butter are one of these flavors combinations that work perfectly. You are going to enjoy this next ice cream flavor.

Serves 12 / Prep. time 15 minutes / Freezing time 4 hours

Ingredients
2 bananas, peeled and diced (plus more for topping, if desired)
¾ cup smooth peanut butter
1 (14-ounce) can sweetened condensed milk
1 teaspoon pure vanilla extract
2 cups heavy cream

Directions
1. In a high-speed blender or food processor, purée the bananas until smooth.
2. In a large mixing bowl mix the condensed milk with the bananas, peanut butter, and vanilla extract.
3. In another bowl, whip the heavy cream until stiff peaks form.
4. Fold a scoop of the whipped cream into the condensed milk mixture, then transfer the sweetened condensed milk mixture into the remaining whipped cream and fold it in until it is creamy and delicious.

5. Spread the mixture in a Pyrex or stainless steel 8x8-inch pan. Spread extra banana slices on top, if desired.
6. Place the ice cream in the freezer for about 4 hours.
7. Remove the ice cream from the freezer and let it stand for 10 minutes.
8. Scoop out and serve.

Nutrition (per serving)
Calories 380, Fat 25.9 g, carbs 31.8 g, sugar 28 g Protein 8.1 g, sodium 129.4 mg

Choco-Coco Ice Cream

If you are a fan of Bounty bars, then you are going to love this chocolate and coconut flavored ice cream. It's easy to make and very delicious.

Serves 12 I Prep. time 15 minutes I Freezing time 4 hours

Ingredients
¾ cup cocoa powder
¾ cup canned coconut milk
1 (14-ounce) can sweetened condensed milk
1 teaspoon pure vanilla extract
2 cups heavy cream

Directions
1. In a large mixing bowl, combine the cocoa powder, coconut milk, condensed milk, and vanilla extract.
2. In another bowl, whip the heavy cream until stiff peaks form.
3. Fold a scoop of the whipped cream into the condensed milk mixture, then transfer the sweetened condensed milk mixture into the remaining whipped cream and fold it in until it is creamy and delicious.
4. Spread the mixture in a Pyrex or stainless steel 8x8-inch pan.
5. Place the ice cream in the freezer for about 4 hours.

6. Remove the ice cream from the freezer and let it stand for 10 minutes.
7. Scoop out and serve.

Nutrition (per serving)
Calories 295, Fat 19.9 g, carbs 27 g, sugar 24.3 g
Protein 5.1 g, sodium 60 mg

Coffee and Oreo® Ice Cream

This next flavor combination is to die for – Oreo and coffee! It's very refreshing and super yummy.

Serves 12 / Prep. time 15 minutes / Freezing time 4 hours

Ingredients
¾ cup brewed espresso
1 (14-ounce) can sweetened condensed milk
1 teaspoon pure vanilla extract
2 cups heavy cream
15 Oreo cookies, crushed

Directions
1. In a large mixing bowl, combine the espresso with the condensed milk and vanilla extract.
2. In another bowl, whip the heavy cream until stiff peaks form.
3. Fold a scoop of the whipped cream into the condensed milk mixture, then transfer the sweetened condensed milk mixture into the remaining whipped cream and fold it in until it is creamy and delicious.
4. Spread the mixture in a Pyrex or stainless steel 8x8-inch pan.
5. Place the ice cream in the freezer for about 2 hours.

6. Fold in the crushed cookies, and return to the freezer for 2 more hours.
7. Remove the ice cream from the freezer and let it stand for 10 minutes.
8. Scoop out and serve.

Nutrition (per serving)
Calories 335, Fat 20.6 g, carbs 34.6 g, sugar 30 g
Protein 4.2 g, sodium 123.9 mg

Raspberry Cheesecake Ice Cream

This cheesecake-inspired ice cream recipe is bursting with raspberry flavor, and you are going to ask for more.

Serves 12 I Prep. time 15 minutes I Freezing time 4 hours

Ingredients
7 ounces cream cheese, softened
1 (14-ounce) can sweetened condensed milk
1 teaspoon pure vanilla extract
2 cups heavy cream
1 cup raspberry jam

Directions
1. In a large mixing bowl, combine the cream cheese with the condensed milk and vanilla extract.
2. In another bowl, whip the heavy cream until stiff peaks form.
3. Fold a scoop of the whipped cream into the condensed milk mixture, then transfer the sweetened condensed milk mixture into the remaining whipped cream and fold it in until it is creamy and delicious.
4. Spread the mixture in a Pyrex or stainless steel 8x8-inch pan.
5. Place the ice cream in the freezer for about 2 hours.

6. Fold in the raspberry jam, making decorative swirls, and return to the freezer for 2 more hours.
7. Remove the ice cream from the freezer and let it stand for 10 minutes.
8. Scoop out and serve.

Nutrition (per serving)
Calories 391, Fat 23.4 g, carbs 42 g, sugar 40.8 g
Protein 5.0 g, sodium 104 mg

Almond and Honey Ice Cream

If you enjoy nougat, you'll love the original taste of this ice cream.

Serves 12 I Prep. time 10 minutes I Freezing time 4 hours

Ingredients
¼ cup honey
1 (14-ounce) can sweetened condensed milk
1 teaspoon pure vanilla extract
2 cups heavy cream
¾ cup chopped roasted almonds

Directions
1. In a large mixing bowl, combine the honey with the condensed milk and vanilla extract.
2. In another bowl, whip the heavy cream until stiff peaks form.
3. Fold a scoop of the whipped cream into the condensed milk mixture, then transfer the sweetened condensed milk mixture into the remaining whipped cream and fold it in until it is creamy and delicious.
4. Spread the mixture in a Pyrex or stainless steel 8x8-inch pan.
5. Place the ice cream in the freezer for about 2 hours.

6. Fold the chopped almonds into the ice cream base and return it to the freezer for 2 more hours.
7. Remove the ice cream from the freezer and let it stand for 10 minutes.
8. Scoop out and serve.

Nutrition (per serving)
Calories 328, Fat 21 g, carbs 31.4 g, sugar 30.3 g
Protein 5.3 g, sodium 55.4 mg

Honey and Date Ice Cream

Fruity and with a slightly floral taste from the honey, this ice cream recipe is super delicious, easy to make, and full of flavor.

Serves 12 I Prep. time 15 minutes I Freezing time 4 hours

Ingredients
¼ cup honey
1 (14-ounce) can sweetened condensed milk
1 teaspoon pure vanilla extract
2 cups heavy cream
½ cup finely chopped dates

Directions
1. In a large mixing bowl, combine the honey, sweetened condensed milk, and vanilla extract.
2. In another bowl, whip the heavy cream until stiff peaks form.
3. Fold a scoop of the whipped cream into the condensed milk mixture, then transfer the sweetened condensed milk mixture into the remaining whipped cream and fold it in until it is creamy and delicious.
4. Spread the mixture in a Pyrex or stainless steel 8x8-inch pan.
5. Place the ice cream in the freezer for about 2 hours.

6. Take the ice cream out and fold the dates into the base. Return it to the freezer for another 2 hours.
7. Remove the ice cream from the freezer and let it stand for 10 minutes.
8. Scoop out and serve.

Nutrition (per serving)
Calories 304, Fat 17.7 g, carbs 33.8 g, sugar 34 g
Protein 4.0 g, sodium 55.4 mg

Pineapple Ginger Ice Cream

This tropical flavor is lightly refreshing with a perfect hint of ginger. It will keep you cool on hot summer days.

Serves 12 I Prep. time 15 minutes I Freezing time 4 hours

Ingredients
¼ cup pineapple juice (from the can)
2 teaspoons grated ginger
1 (14-ounce) can sweetened condensed milk
1 teaspoon pure vanilla extract
2 cups heavy cream
1 cup crushed pineapple, drained

Directions
1. In a large mixing bowl, combine the pineapple juice, ginger, sweetened condensed milk, and vanilla extract.
2. In another bowl, whip the heavy cream until stiff peaks form.
3. Fold a scoop of the whipped cream into the condensed milk mixture, then transfer the sweetened condensed milk mixture into the remaining whipped cream and fold it in until it is creamy and delicious.
4. Spread the mixture in a Pyrex or stainless steel 8x8-inch pan.

5. Place the ice cream in the freezer for about 2 hours.
6. Take the ice cream out and stir the pineapple into the base. Return it to the freezer for another 2 hours.
7. Remove the ice cream from the freezer and let it stand for 10 minutes.
8. Scoop out and serve.

Nutrition (per serving)
Calories 281, Fat 17.7 g, carbs 27.5 g, sugar 27 g
Protein 3.9 g, sodium 55.4 mg

Copycat Cherry Garcia Ice Cream

Cherries and chocolate? Yes, please! You're going to love this copycat recipe inspired by the original.

Serves 12 / Prep. time 15 minutes / Freezing time 4 hours

Ingredients
1 (14-ounce) can sweetened condensed milk
1 teaspoon vanilla extract
2 cups heavy cream
4 ounces dark chocolate, finely grated
2 cups dark cherries, pitted and chopped

Directions
1. In a large mixing bowl, combine the condensed milk and vanilla extract.
2. In another bowl, whip the chilled heavy cream until stiff peaks form.
3. Take one scoop of the whipped cream and fold it in the condensed milk mixture, then transfer the sweetened condensed milk mixture into the remaining whipped cream. Mix gently until it is creamy and delicious.
4. Pour the ice cream base into a Pyrex or stainless steel 8x8-inch pan, and place it in the freezer for about 2 hours.
5. Remove the pan from the freezer and fold in the chocolate and cherries.

6. Place the pan back in the freezer for about 2 more hours.
7. Remove the ice cream from the freezer and let it stand for 10 minutes.
8. Scoop out and serve.

Nutrition (per serving)
Calories 324, Fat 20.5 g, carbs 33 g, sugar 31.2 g
Protein 4.5 g, sodium 58.5 mg

Caramel Chunk Ice Cream

Get ready to give out this recipe! As soon as people taste this ice cream, they'll want to know how to make it.

Serves 12 I Prep. time 15 minutes I Freezing time 4 hours

Ingredients
1 (14-ounce) can sweetened condensed milk
1 teaspoon pure vanilla extract
2 cups heavy cream
½ cup caramel sundae sauce
1 Caramilk® bar, chopped

Directions
1. In a large mixing bowl, combine the condensed milk and vanilla extract.
2. In another bowl, whip the heavy cream until stiff peaks form.
3. Take a scoop of the whipped cream and fold it into the condensed milk mixture, then transfer the sweetened condensed milk mixture into the remaining whipped cream. Mix gently.
4. Pour the base into a Pyrex or stainless steel 8x8-inch pan, and freeze for about 2 hours

5. Remove the pan from the freezer. Fold in the chopped candy bar, and create swirls with the sauce.
6. Place the ice cream back in the freezer for about 2 more hours.
7. Remove the ice cream from the freezer and let it stand for 10 minutes.
8. Scoop out and serve.

Nutrition (per serving)
Calories 362, Fat 18.8 g, carbs 26.9 g, sugar 26 g Protein 4.0 g, sodium 59.7 mg

SUNDAE SAUCES

Chocolate Sundae Sauce

This is amazingly delicious chocolate sundae sauce that everyone will enjoy. It's easy to make with the simplest of ingredients and everyone will love the rich chocolate flavor.

Serves 6 / Prep. time 10 minutes / Cooking time 14-16 minutes

Ingredients
2 tablespoons butter
½ cup granulated sugar
½ cup dark cocoa powder
¼ cup water
1 teaspoon vanilla extract

Directions
1. In a saucepan over medium heat, melt the butter and stir in the sugar, cocoa powder, and water.
2. Bring it to a boil and let it simmer on low for a few minutes. Remove it from the heat and stir in the vanilla extract.
3. Transfer the sauce in a jar or pitcher and serve it hot or cold.

Nutrition (per serving)
Calories 112, Fat 4.3 g, carbs 18.7 g, sugar 16.8 g
Protein 0.7 g, sodium 28 mg

Caramel Sundae Sauce

This is a traditional sundae sauce that everyone makes for topping their ice cream. You will enjoy my twist on this delicious sauce.

Serves 6 I Prep. time 10 minutes I Cooking time 10 minutes

Ingredients
¾ cup granulated sugar
⅓ cup unsalted butter
½ cup heavy cream
Pinch of salt
½ teaspoon almond extract

Directions
1. In a saucepan over medium heat, melt the sugar until it is golden brown.
2. Immediately stir in the butter and heavy cream, and mix until smooth.
3. Season with a pinch of salt and almond extract.
4. Transfer the sauce to a jar or pitcher and serve it hot or cold.

Nutrition (per serving)
Calories 253, Fat 17.5 g, carbs 25.6 g, sugar 26 g
Protein 0.5 g, sodium 8.9 mg

Peanut Butter Sundae Sauce

If you crave something decadent to top your ice cream, then this peanut butter sauce is the thing for you.

Serves 6 / Prep. time 10 minutes / Cooking time 4-6 minutes

Ingredients
½ cup sweetened condensed milk
½ cup creamy peanut butter
6 tablespoons water
1 teaspoon vanilla extract

Directions
1. In a saucepan over medium heat, combine the peanut butter and sweetened condensed milk.
2. Cook the whole mixture until everything is melted, and then stir in the water and let it cook for about 4-6 minutes.
3. Stir in the vanilla.
4. Transfer the sauce in a jar or pitcher to cool completely.
5. Serve on top of the ice cream immediately, or microwave it later to use again.

Nutrition (per serving)
Calories 215, Fat 12.7 g, carbs 20.8 g, sugar 17 g
Protein 6.7 g, sodium 120 mg

Strawberry Sundae Sauce

If you crave something fruity to top your ice cream, then you are going to love this next recipe.

Serves 6 I Prep. time 10 minutes I Cooking time 10 minutes

Ingredients
2 cups fresh strawberries, stemmed and halved
½ cup granulated sugar
1 tablespoon cornstarch
1 tablespoon lemon juice

Directions
1. In a saucepan over medium heat, combine the strawberries and granulated sugar.
2. Cook the whole mixture until the juices are released and the strawberries are soft.
3. Combine the cornstarch and lemon juice and stir the mixture into the strawberries. Cook for 4-10 minutes, until thickened.
4. Transfer the sauce to a jar or pitcher, and serve it hot or cold.

Nutrition (per serving)
Calories 84, fat 0.2 g, carbs 21.6 g, sugar 19.1 g
Protein 0.3 g, sodium 1 mg

Banana Sundae Sauce

This banana sundae sauce is something your ice cream wants you to top it with. Serve it as a special treat.

Serves 6 / Prep. time 10 minutes / Cooking time 10 minutes

Ingredients
½ cup butter
1 ½ cups icing sugar
1 tablespoon water
1 teaspoon lemon juice
1 teaspoon vanilla extract
2 bananas, cut in pieces

Directions
1. In a saucepan over medium heat, melt the butter and stir in the icing sugar, water, lemon juice, and vanilla extract.
2. Finally, stir in the banana pieces and let them cook for 2–3 minutes.
3. Let the mixture cool a bit, and then purée it until smooth.
4. Transfer the sauce to a jar or pitcher and serve it warm or cold.

Nutrition (per serving)
Calories 290, Fat 15.5 g, carbs 39 g, sugar 34.3 g Protein 0.6 g, sodium 110 mg

HOMEMADE CONES AND ICE CREAM SANDWICH COOKIES

Homemade Ice Cream Cone

Making homemade ice cream cones is the most fun part of eating ice cream. It's easy and super delicious.

Serves 8 / Prep. time 10 minutes / Cooking time 4-6 minutes

Ingredients
2 large eggs, room temperature
½ cup granulated sugar
¼ cup butter, melted
3 tablespoons whole milk
½ teaspoon vanilla extract
⅓ cup all-purpose flour
3 tablespoons vegetable oil

Directions
1. Form a cone shape using aluminum foil, ensuring that it is firm.
2. In a large mixing bowl, whisk the eggs with the granulated sugar until frothy.
3. Beat in the butter, milk, vanilla extract, flour, and oil. The mixture should be thin.
4. Heat a small skillet over medium heat, and brush it lightly with oil.

5. Pour ¼ cup of the batter into the pan and spread it by moving the pan in a circle. When the underside is brown in color, flip it and cook for a minute or so on the other side so you get nice golden-brown color.
6. Remove the water from the pan and place in on a work surface or cutting board.
7. To form the cone shape, fold the upper part of the wafer over the form and press firmly at the tip to create a seal. Roll the cone over slowly until the shape is complete. Hold the cone firmly in place, seam side down, until it is cool enough to maintain its own shape. It will take about 30-40 seconds.
8. Serve with your favorite ice cream recipe.

Nutrition (per serving)
Calories 184, Fat 12 g, carbs 16.9 g, sugar 12.9 g
Protein 2.4 g, sodium 61 mg

Perfect Waffle Cone

If you have an ice cream cone machine, but you haven't used it since you bought it, I think now is time to make this perfect ice cream cone recipe.

Serves 8 / Prep. time 10 minutes / Cooking time 4-6 minutes

Ingredients
2 egg whites
½ cup granulated sugar
5 tablespoons butter, melted
⅓ cup heavy cream
1 teaspoon vanilla extract
⅔ cup all-purpose flour

Directions
1. In a large mixing bowl, whisk the egg whites with the granulated sugar until frothy.
2. Stir in the butter, cream, vanilla extract, and flour.
3. Heat an ice cream cone waffle maker.
4. Pour ¼ cup of the batter in the machine and close the lid of the waffle maker.
5. Cook for 2–3 minutes, until golden.
6. Immediately, while the waffle is still hot, form the cone shape. Fold the upper part of the waffle over the form and press firmly at the tip to create a seal. Roll the waffle over slowly to form the cone.

7. Hold the waffle cone firmly in place, seam side down, until it is cool enough to maintain its own shape. This will take 30–40 seconds.
9. Serve with your favorite ice cream recipe.

Nutrition (per serving)
Calories 172, Fat 9.2 g, carbs 20.7 g, sugar 12.7 g
Protein 2.2 g, sodium 62 mg

Chocolate Cookies for Ice Cream Sandwiches

Who doesn't like ice cream sandwiches? With this recipe, no need to ever get store-bought!

*Serves 12 / Prep. time 30 minutes /
Cooking time 10 minutes /
Freezing time 30-60 minutes*

Ingredients

Other ingredients

6 tablespoons unsalted butter, softened
1 teaspoon pure vanilla extract
½ cup white sugar
¼ light brown sugar
⅔ cup whole milk
Cooking spray or butter for greasing
Vanilla ice cream

Dry ingredients

1 ¼ cups all-purpose flour
½ cup cocoa
½ teaspoon baking soda
½ teaspoon kosher salt

Directions

1. Preheat the oven to 350°F and place the oven rack into the middle position.

2. Grease lightly a piece of parchment paper, about 12"x16" with butter or cooking spray, and set aside flat in a large baking sheet. Set aside
3. In the bowl of a stand mixer, set with the whisk attachment, cream the butter, vanilla, and white and brown sugars until fluffy, about 2 minutes on medium speed.
4. Reduce speed to low and add in 3 increments the dry ingredients and the milk. Beat until well incorporated between each addition and with a spatula, scrape the sides of the bowl.
5. Spread the batter evenly over the parchment paper
6. Bake in the oven for 10 minutes. Remove the pan from the oven and allow cooling for 4-6 minutes. Cut it in half to make two long rectangles of 6" x 16".
7. Prick the top of the cookie pieces evenly with a fork to look like a store-bought ice cream sandwich.
8. Arrange both cookie pieces, with their parchment on the bottom, on wired racks to cool completely.
9. When completely cooled down, wrap each cookie piece with plastic wrap and place them on the baking sheet and place in the freezer
10. When you are ready to make the ice cream sandwich, remove the baking sheet

from the freezer. Peel off the parchment paper from both cookie pieces. Place one cookie piece bottom up. Spread with vanilla ice cream. Top with the second cookie piece, top side up. Push down to disperse the ice cream evenly between the cookie pieces.

11. Cut the edges of the sandwiches to make them pretty. If the ice cream starts to soften too much, place the baking sheet back in the freezer to harden, about 30-60 minutes. Once firm, cut into 12 even sandwiches.
12. Eat immediately; or wrap each sandwich in plastic wrap, and store in the freezer. They will keep fresh up to 2 months.

RECIPE INDEX

CLASSIC FLAVORS   **3**
  Vanilla Ice Cream   3
  Chocolate Ice Cream   5
  Strawberry Ice Cream   7
  Butter Pecan Ice Cream   9
  Coffee Ice Cream   11
  Coconut Ice Cream   13
  Chocolate Chip Ice Cream   15
  Maple Walnut Ice Cream   17
  Birthday Cake Ice Cream   19
  Peanut Butter Ice Cream   21
  Neapolitan Ice Cream   23
  Pistachio Ice Cream   25
  Chocolate Chip Cookie Dough Ice Cream   27
  Mint and Chocolate Chip Ice Cream   29

FRUIT-BASED FLAVORS   **31**
  Blackberry Lime Ice Cream   31
  Raspberry and Chocolate Ice Cream   33
  Pear Ice Cream   35
  Apple Caramel Ice Cream   37
  Honey Ice Cream   39
  Chocolate Chips Ice Cream   41
  Date Ice Cream   43
  Almond Butter Ice Cream   45
  Cherry Ice Cream   47
  Plum Chip Ice Cream   49
  Dried Fig Ice Cream   51
  Banana Bread Ice Cream   53
  Cherry Ice Cream   55
  Blueberry Lemon Ice Cream   57
  Creamy Orange Ice Cream   59
  Strawberry and Graham Cracker Ice Cream   61

Lemon and Poppy Seed Ice Cream	63
Papaya Tropics Ice Cream	65

NEW FLAVORS 67

Cereal Ice Cream	67
Pecans and Molasses Ice Cream	69
Marshmallow Ice Cream	71
Greek Yoghurt and Maple Syrup Ice Cream	73
Chai Ice Cream	75
PB and J Ice Cream	77
Cinnamon French Toast Ice Cream	79

COMBINATION FLAVORS 81

Chocolate and Hazelnut Ice Cream	81
Almond Butter Ice Cream	83
Peanut Butter and Chocolate Chip Ice Cream	85
Peanut Butter and Banana Ice Cream	87
Choco-Coco Ice Cream	89
Coffee and Oreo® Ice Cream	91
Raspberry Cheesecake Ice Cream	93
Almond and Honey Ice Cream	95
Honey and Date Ice Cream	97
Pineapple Ginger Ice Cream	99
Copycat Cherry Garcia Ice Cream	101
Caramel Chunk Ice Cream	103

SUNDAE SAUCES 105

Chocolate Sundae Sauce	105
Caramel Sundae Sauce	107
Peanut Butter Sundae Sauce	108
Strawberry Sundae Sauce	109
Banana Sundae Sauce	110

HOMEMADE CONES AND ICE CREAM SANDWICH COOKIES 111

Homemade Ice Cream Cone	111
Perfect Waffle Cone	113
Chocolate Cookies for Ice Cream Sandwiches	115

Printed in Great Britain
by Amazon